Dash The Turtle Lives in The Grass

Look Around on The Ground

Just beneath the surface of the grass lives a small green turtle named Dash.

His mother named him Dash when hatched from an egg. Dash crawled so fast he looked like he ran on one leg.

Dash is happy and plays all the time and helps his friends like Mr. Frog, and Ms. Rabbit, understand why.

Dash loves going to school and play adventures outside.

Like treasure hunting, running, jumping, and flying a kite.

But most important when playing hide-and-seek is stay away from playing in the street. Dash and his friends could get hurt so when playing outside stay alert.

STOP

DO NOT PLAY IN THE STREET

Dash helps his friends when they are angry or mad, grumpy, pouty or even sad.

His happiness spreads cheer and brightens everyone's day, so why would Dash want to feel any other way.

"I'm a happy, happy, turtle who dashes all over the place, and I enjoy spreading happiness, you can see it on my face."

"Why Mr. Frog and Ms. Rabbit ask, why are you always happy and never sad?" You live in a hole just beneath the grass.

Dash says to his friends, "I love living in a hole just beneath the grass, I cannot help but be happy it's who I am, I get to live and play with my family and friends."

Dash says to his family and friends, "I'm a happy, happy, turtle who dashes all over the place, and I enjoy spreading happiness, you can see it on my face."

I get to play outside and I have many friends such as Mr. Frog, and Ms. Rabbit, Royce the mouse, and Ms. Betty the hen.

Being grumpy, pouty, angry and sad makes me and my friends feel like mud which taste really bad.

There are many days and times when I feel angry or mad, grumpy, pouty or even sad.

Especially when I do things mom and dad say not to do.

Mom and Dad Rules
1. No playing in the street
2. Come straight home after school
3. Pick up toys
4. Be kind to others

Like not putting my toys away and playing with glue or play where I shouldn't play and not coming home right after school.

But talking to my family and friends like Mr. Frog, Ms. Rabbit or Ms. Betty the hen makes me feel happy inside again.

Dash the green turtle is happy and positive all the time. He helps his friends be happy and not angry or mad, not even grumpy, pouty or even sad. By talking with friends and family Dash and friends learn an important lesson about emotions.

51654560R00015

Made in the USA
Middletown, DE
13 November 2017